Walking with God:
Enjoying God's Presence from Morning to Night

Walking with God

ENJOYING GOD'S PRESENCE
FROM MORNING TO NIGHT

ASHERITAH CIUCIU

Cover design by Flaviu Ciuciu

Proofreading by Vicki Caswell

Author photograph by Ashley McCom

Table of Contents

For Mom:
Thank you for modeling what it looks like to
faithfully walk with God in all seasons of life.
You're the best mother a girl could ask for, and
the most wonderful mentor and friend.

Introduction

If you've ever felt a disconnect between your daily devotions and the rest of your day, you know that empty feeling. There's got to be something more to the Christian life than checking off a Bible reading plan and going to church on Sunday. …Right?

There is.

When God calls us to Himself, He's not pulling us into a room and asking us to stay put until Kingdom come. He's inviting us to join Him on the journey of a lifetime, to experience His presence in every area of our life, and to see how He is moving in and around the world.

Too often we get stuck in a spiritual rut and despair of ever experiencing the richness of a dynamic relationship with Jesus. But spiritual intimacy is not reserved for an elite few—it's available to everyone who seeks God with all their hearts. And it's beautifully portrayed in the metaphor of a walk.

Walking with God: Enjoying God's Presence from Morning to Night is meant to help bridge the gap between daily devotions and the rest of our time. By exploring the metaphor of a walk, we will learn how our relationship with God is like a walk, how God has walked with people differently throughout history, how we can overcome spiritual roadblocks, and how we can go deeper in our walks through spiritual disciplines.

Each day's reading in this four-week study is set up in two parts: a devotional that will help you think about walking with God in a different light and a response section that will help you apply the teaching to your life.

My heart desire is that this book will help you discover deeper intimacy with God as you learn to walk with Him. May you experience the joy of His presence from the moment you wake up to the moment you go to sleep and every moment in between.

Many blessings,

Asheritah

Week 1:
Rudiments of Walking with God

There needs be neither art nor science
for going to GOD, but only
a heart resolutely determined to apply itself
to nothing but Him, or for His sake,
and to love Him only.
— Brother Lawrence

Exploring the Metaphor
of a Walk

*"Two [disciples] were going to a village called
Emmaus, about seven miles from Jerusalem. They
were talking with each other about everything that
had happened. As they talked and discussed these
things with each other, Jesus himself came up and
walked along with them. Luke 24:13-15*

One of the most famous walks in history happened with little
fanfare and almost by happenstance. Jesus joined two of his
disciples in a walk from Jerusalem to their village, and they
shared the most riveting conversation as Jesus revealed how
all prophesies had been fulfilled in Him, though the disciples
didn't recognize Him even as He was walking alongside
them. How I wish I could have been a fly on their backpacks
to listen in on their conversation! It must have been
fascinating. *Ex: my children - I can spend time w/
them, but not be investing myself in them*

The metaphor of a walk is used throughout Scripture to
describe the relationship God desires to have with His
people Before we look at practical ways to walk with God, *6/21*
let's explore the metaphor of a walk. Why did God choose to
use the imagery of two people walking side-by-side, and what
can we learn about our relationship with God by looking at
this imagery? *Intentionally!*

My husband and I enjoy going on evening strolls together. As
we step away from our house, there's an air of expectation,
knowing that no matter how long or short this stroll will be,
we'll have some time together. I'll ask my husband about his
day, highs and lows, and what's currently on his mind. I'll

listen carefully as he shares about disappointments or surprises at work, on the road, at church, or in his circle of friends. Sometimes I'll interrupt with a question or a comment, and sometimes we jump from one topic to another, comfortably changing subjects even as we change our pace. At times, we stroll in amiable silence, taking in the scenery and happy to simply enjoy each other's company without words. Without conscious thought, we keep pace with each other, automatically adjusting our stride if one of us needs to slow down or speed up. We feel free to interrupt storytelling to point out oddities around us, and we share laughs and inside jokes that no onlooker would understand unless they would have been part of our evening strolls all along.

There's a special camaraderie we share in going on these walks together night after night. They may not be exciting date nights or exotic travel destinations, but they're special precisely in their routineness. Similarly, our relationships with God may not seem remarkable because we're not in a state of constant spiritual euphoria. But our walk with God is just that—a journey that takes place one small step at a time, day after day, hour after hour, mundane minute by mundane minute. *kind of like the time w our family*
But must be intentional

There are several ingredients required for a pleasant walk, and we can use the acronym W.A.L.K. to remember and apply them in our own walks with God:

- Willingness
- Awareness
- Listening

- Keeping pace

Like a couple on an evening stroll, we get to experience close intimacy with God as we walk with Him through life. But unlike the two disciples traveling to Emmaus, we know who our Companion is, and as we rejoice in the privilege of His presence, our lives take on new meaning.

Respond

What comes to mind when you think of walking with God?

Togetherness, not alone, the garden, action word, not just sitting, a choice we make,

"The grass is greener where you water it"

In what ways is our relationship with God similar to a couple on an evening stroll? In what ways is it different?

It's a relationship, a back + forth, a sharing, takes effort, a choice, diff - no waiting for walking w/ God, God already knows all - God always available for a walk

List the different people in the Bible you know of that walked with God, whether in the Old or New Testament. What did they all have in common?

Enoch, David, Isaiah, Ruth, Naomi, Esther, Rahab, Peter, Paul, Mary, Hosea, Abraham, Noah, Jonah, Daniel

- had obedience, faith, walked w/ God - had relationship w/ Him

_____

_____

As we embark on this journey of walking with God, write a prayer asking God to open your heart and help you learn how to walk with Him. Then thank Him for inviting you to walk with Him.

_____

_____

_____

_____

_____

_____

Growing in Willingness and Wonder

I will walk among you and be your God, and you
will be my people. Leviticus 26:12

It's mind-boggling to think that God Himself desires to walk with mere mortals. From Adam and Eve's strolls in the Garden of Eden to Noah and Enoch to David and the disciples and the first-century church, we have lots of examples in the Bible of people walking with God. But before we dig into what that looks like, let's pause to consider the magnitude of even having the possibility of walking with God.

God Himself—the Creator of Heaven and Earth, the One who existed before time and in whom all things hold together—God desires to walk with you and me. Wow. That's all at once exhilarating and humbling. That He desires to walk with us should be enough motivation for us to do whatever it takes to join Him and walk with Him.

But it takes two people to walk together. We've already seen that God wants to walk with us, but we, for our part, must be willing as well.

Walking with God requires willingness. We must be deliberate in seeking God with all our hearts, not because He hides from us but because we have a striking proclivity to turn our backs on Him. We must purpose in our hearts to abandon competing pursuits, following hard after Him and staying close to His side.

A deep relationship with God does not happen by accident; it requires great intentionality because we so often walk aimlessly away from Him. Aware of this sad state of his heart, Robert Robinson penned this beautiful prayer nestled in the well-loved hymn "Come Thou Fount":

> *"Let Thy goodness, like a fetter,*
> *Bind my wandering heart to Thee.*
> *Prone to wander, Lord, I feel it*
> *Prone to leave the God I love;*
> *Here's my heart, O take and seal it*
> *Seal it for Thy courts above."*

May that become our prayer, as we seek to grow in our willingness to walk more closely with our God today and every day. As we grow from wandering to willing walking partners, we will enjoy spiritual renewal, personal transformation, and increased awareness and enjoyment of God's presence.

And what a beautiful way to live this life on earth—walking with our Creator God!

Respond

What does Leviticus 26:12 say about God's desire to walk with His people?

He wants to be with us and walk among us. But we have to walk w/ Him - away

Does that surprise you in any way?

Yes - its hard to understand why
God wants to walk with me?

In your own life, do you feel like God desires to walk with you personally? Why or why not?

It depends when asked! Sometimes
I do, but its when I am in a place
of obedience to Him + reading the Word
that I feel that most

In what ways have you wandered in your relationship with God? How did God respond to you?

By getting away from my time in
the Word - He is always gentle +
draws me back - sometimes by
Chastening

Take a few moments to sing or pray the words of the hymn quoted in today's devotional, making them your prayer to God. Recommit yourself to abandoning other distractions and walking with God.

Ugh - distractions - so hard
to focus! Why I want to
get up earlier + go to bed
earlier

Exchanging Formulas for Awareness

Blessed are those who have learned to acclaim you,
who walk in the light of your presence, Lord.
Psalm 89:15

I've always loved baking. There's a special comfort in knowing that if you follow directions for a recipe to the smallest detail, you'll get yummy goodness. Every. Single. Time.

It's no wonder most of us rely on formulas. They're comforting in their exactness. There's no guessing or wondering how something will turn out. And often we use the same mindset in our relationships with God. We want a 1-2-3 formula for connecting with God. It's easy to think, "If I read the Bible every morning and spend at least 10 minutes praying, and go to church on Sunday, then I'll be spiritually healthy and God will be pleased." We seek to reduce the mystery of a relationship with Almighty God to a simple three-step plan, because that gives us more control over the process and outcome.

But God is not a product—He is a person. And He longs for us to connect with Him, to desire Him, to yearn for Him, and to want to be in relationship with Him throughout the day. This is not a matter of merely "doing our devotions" or ticking off the boxes to impress God. Walking with God is about experiencing deep spiritual intimacy with our Creator. And it requires an awareness of His presence that extends into every facet of our lives.

In Psalm 89, we learn that those who have learned to acclaim God walk in His presence. As we worship God in our private moments of devotion, He reveals Himself to us in deeper and more significant ways, which changes us both in that moment and during the rest of our day. We cannot experience the presence of God and leave unchanged; we carry that awareness of His presence into the rest of our day.

Just as it would be rude of me to go on a walk with my husband but be glued to my phone screen the whole time, living the Christian life but ignoring God's presence is equally inconsiderate. He wants us to share the journey with Him, to delight in Him, and to grow in intimate relationship with Him.

There is no easy formula because this is a dynamic relationship. As we seek God, we will find Him when we seek Him with all our hearts; He will allow Himself to be found by us (Jeremiah 29:13) and in His presence we will experience the fullness of joy (Psalm 16:11). And that experience, friends, is better than any bakery delicacy.

Respond

In what ways do formulas and checklists provide comfort for a given task? What's their biggest limitation?

Stability, knowing what come next, predictability

Sometime had to adjust or think about the plan, more cause frustration or reduce spontaneity

Have you ever been tempted to reduce spirituality to a formula in your own life? Why do you think this is? What did it look like?

Yes, definitely - some a result of upbringing and making life a list of rules + don'ts produces guilt

What does our desire for formulas say about our approach to spirituality?

Well, it may say that we think of spirituality as a to-do list instead of a relationship + life style

Rewrite Psalm 89:15 in first person, inserting your name.

Blessed am I who has learned to acclaim you, who will in the light of your presence, Lord.

Write a prayer asking God to help you <u>break free from a</u> formula mentality and begin pursuing a relationship with Him that reaches into every corner of your life and every moment of your day.

Learning to Listen to God

Therefore, as you received Christ Jesus the Lord,
so walk in him. Colossians 2:6 (ESV)

Throughout the book of Colossians, Paul talks about the importance of an intimate, spiritual, and living union with Christ. As we've already seen, being a Christian isn't just making a one-time vow of allegiance—it's a continuous choice to walk with Jesus each day.

The word Paul uses to describe the act of walking means to regulate one's life and comes from a root word meaning to advance, to move forward, and to trample underfoot. It's the imagery of putting one foot in front of the other as we press on toward a goal, all while being mindful of surrounding circumstances. This requires active listening

So in our walk with God, we must practice active listening. According to Colossians 2:7, we listen in our walk with God in three ways:

Listening to His Voice

Those who belong to God have the Spirit of God living within us, and He is eager to share His thoughts with us as we become "rooted and built up in Him" (see also 1 Corinthians 2:16). So as we run errands, file reports, grocery shop, and care for our families, we must practice listening to Him. Is there someone He wants us to talk to? Perhaps there's someone He wants to love through our actions? Or maybe He wants us to pause on our commute home and admire His artistry at work in the sunset? Let's not be so preoccupied with our activities that we drown out His voice.

Obeying His Direction

Not only does the Spirit of God accompany us in our daily activities, but He also longs to guide us, "strengthening us in the faith" as we obey His lead. Throughout Scripture we see examples of women and men who changed course because they listened to God, and they (and those around them) were blessed by their obedience. Sadly, we also have examples of those who disobeyed and chose to go their own direction (Jonah, anyone?), and the results are always disastrous. Seek His guidance before making decisions, and be sensitive to promptings to pause and pray before rushing into things. Often those promptings are our walking partner elbowing us and saying, "This is the way. Walk in it" (Isaiah 30:21).

Sharing Our Own Reflections

Lastly, we practice active listening by responding to God's Spirit, "overflowing with thankfulness." As we go about our day, let us share our hearts with God, keeping in constant communication with Him. We are blessed with thousands of gifts every day; what a joy it is to rejoice over those with God, thanking Him for every little blessing, savoring those "coincidences" that we know only come from Him, looking for His mercy when we're frustrated or asking for His fruit in our lives when we feel like we're going to lose our temper. God delights in us when we share our hearts with Him, and the mundane becomes sacred when done with thanksgiving.

Be encouraged that listening in our walk with God becomes easier the more often we do it, as seventeenth-century monk Brother Lawrence shares in his book, *The Practice of the Presence of God*:

Let [us] then think of God as much as possible so that [we] will gradually become accustomed to this little but holy exercise; no one will notice it and nothing is easier than to repeat often during the day these little acts of interior adoration.

As we learn to listen to the voice of God, follow the direction of God, and share our thoughts with God, we grow closer to Him, and He delights in us as we walk with Him.

Respond

What does Colossians 2:6-7 say about the Christian life after the moment of conversion?

to continue to live in Him, rooted
& built up, strengthened in the faith
overflowing with thankfulness

Of the three aspects of walking with God listed in this passage (listening to God's voice, obeying God's direction, and sharing your reflections), which is the most difficult for you? Why?

Listening - being still
enough to hear His voice

In what ways can you practice active listening today so that you may walk more closely with God?

Quiet moments - writing out
instructions to listen to His voice

_____

_____

Write a prayer of confession and rededication, asking the
Spirit of Christ to help you walk in Him.

_____

_____

_____

_____

_____

_____

_____

_____

Keeping Pace in Every Place

Even though I walk through the darkest valley, I
will fear no evil, for you are with me. Psalm 23:4

Psalm 23 is one of the most beloved psalms of Christians and
non-Christians alike, and it's probably the most often-quoted
Scripture at funerals. And for good reason. These words
penned by King David are rich truths that sustain us no
matter what season of life we're in.

As any senior citizen, will likely tell you, life is not a straight
line. Each of us will experience both great joys and crippling
pain, exciting rushes of adrenaline and soul-crushing defeat
that leaves us numb and questioning the goodness of God.
We all have stories that we love to tell because they have
fantastic endings, and we probably all have stories we keep
hidden under layers of pleasantries because they leave us
feeling raw, vulnerable, and exposed.

But in the midst of all these moments, right in the midst of
each high and low, God has been walking alongside His
children every step of the way. He is present in the green
hillsides with sparkling brooks just as much as He is present
in the darkest valleys with frightening shadows that threaten
to engulf us. David understood this well. From the quiet
pastures to the bloody battlefields to the palace intrigues,
David knew what it meant to keep in step with God, and he
also knew the devastating effects of rushing ahead of Him.

The truth is that walking with God is not always easy or fun.
In fact, it often requires spiritual, emotional, and mental
energy that leaves us feeling drained, and the difficulty of our
trek makes us wonder if we're on this journey alone. But

make no mistake—God never leaves our side. Like a Good Shepherd, He gently guides His sheep, always within reach, even when we don't see or feel Him. He knows exactly what we need in every season of life, and He graciously walks with us through the good and the bad.

Do not discount the journey. <u>Don't rush ahead</u>, wanting to have all the answers to your unknowns. <u>Savor the process and welcome His direction.</u> It's often in this uncertainty that He reveals something new about His character, and it's in the waiting and the seeking that we draw even closer to Him. So let us keep pace with God.

Let us not dwell on the hardships we've left behind, for He leads us to quiet waters and restores our souls. Let us not rush ahead when we spot lush meadows, for He will take us there in His time. And let us not lag behind for fear of the difficulties coming up, for He is with us and nothing can harm us. All the way our Savior leads us—what else could we ask for?

Whatever season of life we're in right now, we can put one foot in front of the other, knowing that the most loving Companion is with us every step of the way. And He will guide us home.

Respond

Does God seem close to you or far away right now? Why?

Kind of far - because I am
not making time for Him.

In what ways has He reassured you of His presence in the past?

By answering big or small
prayers.
Sometimes happening in a day to remind
me He hears me & loves me

Read Psalm 23 in its entirety. How can the verses in this psalm strengthen your faith in His goodness and help you keep pace with Him in this season?

Which verse best represents your life in this season? Write it on an index card and post it somewhere you will see it every day to remember God's presence in your life.

Write out a prayer expressing your heart to God.

Weekend Reflection

What did you learn about God this week?

_____

_____

_____

_____

_____

_____

What did you learn about yourself this week?

_____

_____

_____

_____

_____

_____

What did you learn about walking with God this week?

_____

_____

_____

_____

_____

Write an honest prayer to God

_____

_____

_____

_____

_____

_____

Notes

Week 2:
Records of Walking with God

*Those who walk with God
always reach their destination.*
— Unknown

Strolling the Garden with God: Adam and Eve

Then the man and his wife heard the sound of the LORD God as he was walking in the garden in the cool of the day, and they hid from the LORD God among the trees of the garden. Genesis 3:8

Some days, I wish I could sit down with Eve and talk with her. I'd love to know what life was like before sin entered the world.

Before Adam and Eve disobeyed God, they dwelled with Him in the Garden of Eden. Unhindered by sin, guilt, shame, or false expectations, all they ever knew was a genuine, intimate experience with their Creator. They met Him in the stillness of the evening as they strolled the Garden together, talking about life as they knew it. God created humans to have a relationship with them, and we can only imagine what that looked like in the early days of our history.

What did they talk about? Did they hike mountains together? Did they swim in the rivers and marvel at God's creatures swimming alongside them? Did they share what had happened in the Garden and in Heaven that day?

We don't know what they did. But we do know that there was continual giving of love and affirmation on both sides. Adam and Eve were constantly thanking God and telling Him how much they enjoyed the life He had given them in the garden. We know this because this is what we're called to do as believers in Christ. Adam and Eve's relationship spoke volumes on the way God loved them, and their unhindered intimacy with each other mirrored the intimacy they enjoyed with their Creator. They were naked. And unashamed.

But with the Fall, their ability to connect with God in such an intimate and unhindered way died, as God had told them would happen. In eating the fruit, Adam and Eve entered death, and they were no longer able to freely enjoy God's presence as they had before.

But in His mercy, God did not banish them completely from His presence. He made a way for them and their descendants to continue a relationship with Him by the spilling of blood. God offered the first sacrifice when He clothed Adam and Eve, foreshadowing the sacrifice of Jesus, the second Adam, who would provide a way for all of humanity to experience the intimacy with God that Adam and Eve had enjoyed in the Garden.

Our journey into the records of walking with God may seem to have a dismal start, but it gets better. Promise.

Respond

What did walking with God look like for Adam and Eve?

Perfect peace, joy, happiness, contentment — no fear or pain, or shame, perfect communion

Picture yourself in the Garden, alongside Adam and Eve as they strolled with God. What would it be like to be unhindered by sin, guilt, and shame? Imagine their conversations. How would they look at God and at each other?

Perfectly, with no judgement or fears - just pure & with complete perfect love

If possible, search online for "Creation's Song--My Heart Belongs to You." Journal your thoughts after listening to that song. Do you agree or disagree with the picture portrayed in the song?

Though Adam and Eve lost the privilege of entering God's presence anytime and anywhere because of their sin, Jesus' death secures for us that privilege today. Spend some time approaching the throne room of God, without fear or trepidation, but full of joy and confidence because He wants you there. Talk to Him as if He were physically next to you, because in a very real way, He is.

Wandering from God: The Israelites

I will establish them and increase their numbers,
and I will put my sanctuary among them forever.
My dwelling place will be with them; I will be their
God, and they will be my people.
Ezekiel 37:26-27

It's easy to read the Old Testament as stories that have nothing to do with us today, but those stories tell us much about God's desire to have a relationship with His people.

After Adam and Eve introduced sin into the world, God promised a rescue plan. Hundreds of years later, He chose one man, Abraham, to be the father of the nation of Israel through which His rescue would come. God made a one-sided promise, called a covenant, with Abraham and his descendants, promising that He would bless the world through the Promised One, the Messiah, who would come from their nation.

But God's promise wasn't just for future blessing; He also wanted the Israelites to walk with Him while they waited for the Messiah. So through Moses He gave them laws to set them apart from the other nations, a system of sacrifices to purify them of their sins, and a call to worship God alone.

In essence, God was saying, "I'm going to fix what is broken in our relationship. These laws and sacrifices are a temporary fix; someday I will send the Messiah and He will make all things right forever. But in the meantime, if you want to walk with Me, you need to keep these commandments."

Simple, right?

But again and again, the Israelites turned away from God and pursued other gods. They thought His laws were too harsh and it seemed like the neighboring countries were having all the fun. To bring them back to Himself, God would send wars, plagues, and devastation, knowing that calamity was the only thing that would cause them to repent and turn to Him. When the Israelites would cry out to God for mercy, He would generously intervene, and all would be well until they wandered from Him again.

The entire Old Testament is one long narrative of the Israelites wandering from God and God faithfully calling them back to Himself, forgiving them, and giving them another chance.

Come to think of it, that sounds a lot like my life story, maybe yours too. What a patient God we serve, that He keeps calling us back to Himself again and again!

Respond

In 1-2 sentences, summarize what walking with God looked like for the Israelites.

Obedience, Walking away, punishment, God bringing them back - over & over over ....

Read Hebrews 11. The Israelites had nothing but rituals and commands to go by, and yet the Old Testament is filled with people whose faith is credited to them as righteousness. Pick three people from the chapter, and list how they walked with

God. How did God reveal Himself to them? What was their relationship with God like?

Noah - God spoke to him, Noah had faith + reverence to R God

Abraham - God called him - had faith

Sarah - God helped her conceive, had faith in God + called Him faithful - Affilled His promise

What stands out to you about the Israelites' history of rebelling against God and returning to Him again?

That God is so patient + kind - always a God of second chances. And H will never go back on His promises + is -

In what ways is your life story similar to the Israelites? What have you learned about God's character so far in your walk with Him?

I keep wandering yet God gently keeps bringing me back. I've learned that God's character is strong + true, and faithful It loves w/ passion + unconditionally

Write a prayer thanking God for His willingness to walk with you and asking Him to help you keep pace with Him.

Thank you, Lord, for never giving up on me - for always helping me get back on track - for loving me and caring for me no matter how many times I ignore you as Lord of my life

Trekking with God Among Us: Emmanuel

*The Word became flesh and made his dwelling
among us. We have seen his glory, the glory of the
one and only Son, who came from the Father, full
of grace and truth.*
John 1:14

All of Israel's history pointed to the time when Jesus would
come and fulfill the many promises of God. He was nothing
like they expected, but He was everything they needed.

When Jesus came, God entered the world in bodily form and
actually dwelled with people. He ate, He talked, He walked,
He laughed, He cried. He selected a group of men and
women to be close to Him, and they did life together,
traveling from village to village to preach the Kingdom of
God.

Jesus befriended the people everyone else rejected: the weak,
the unpopular, the sinful, and the hopeless. Again and again,
Jesus upset the cultural and social norms of the day and
broke religious customs that people had enacted to create a
hierarchy of spirituality. He confronted those who had
changed God's laws into a spiritual checklist and reinforced
that God wanted a relationship with those who recognized
their need for Him.

For the extent of Jesus's earthly ministry, walking with God
was possible in a very unique way that has only happened
then and there. This tiny sliver of human history witnessed

what no one before or after has: God Himself lived on earth. And it was a breathtaking thing.

But what follows is even more incredible: Jesus' work was not only in His teaching and healing ministry. His greatest assignment lay in His voluntary death to pay the penalty for humanity's sins, restoring what became broken with Adam and Eve.

The very people He came to save rejected Him, beat Him, and crucified Him. He died a criminal's death although He was holiness embodied. He died the death we all deserved so that we could walk with Him as He had always wanted. But Jesus did not stay dead; through the power of the Holy Spirit, He defeated death and raised to life, declaring His power and authority over everything in the universe—death included.

No longer would people have to rely on sacrifices, priests, or intercessors to get into God's presence—they could now boldly walk into His throne room through the sacrifice of Jesus. Through His death and resurrection, Jesus threw open the gates of heaven so anyone who believed in Him could have free access to God.

If that doesn't make you stand up and shout, I don't know what will!

Respond

What did walking with God look like for Jesus' disciples?

personal in the flesh. constant teaching moments

What parts of their experience can we share, and what will we have to wait for until we reach heaven?

We can spend time with Jesus
but we don't physically see him
face to face

In what ways is Jesus' ministry on earth the culmination of God's promises in the Old Testament?

fulfilled promise of Messiah,
a sacrifice who did away with all
the sacrifices. Etc to get to His presence

How does Jesus' death and resurrection influence your walk with God today?

Centers me - makes me thankful I
even have the ability to be in
His presence.

Write a prayer praising God for His relentless pursuit of intimacy with humans, even in the face of our continual rejection of Him. Specifically, take time to praise Jesus for the ways He restored your relationship with God.

Keeping In Step with the Spirit: Christians Today

If we live by the Spirit, let us also keep in step with the Spirit. Galatians 5:25

After Jesus ascended to heaven, He sent the disciples the best guide possible: His very Spirit. It would be easy to bemoan the fact that we missed those precious days Jesus spent walking on earth, but Jesus Himself said that it's better for us that He go to heaven so that we may enjoy the presence of the Spirit in our lives (see John 16:7). He has given us His very best!

The Holy Spirit, being in very nature God, was present before the beginning of the world; He moved over the waters at the dawn of creation; He filled people for brief periods of time in the Old Testament, and after Jesus' ascension, He took on a permanent role in believers' lives. He is the One Jesus promised to send us, to teach, help, guide, and comfort us (John 14:26). He is the guarantee we cling to that all God's promises will come true, because He is the seal of salvation (Ephesians 1:14).

Though it may sometimes seem that walking with God is a mysterious discipline or we're left on our own to try to "figure it out," the truth is that God is right by our side, eager to instruct us and teach us the way should go (Psalm 32:8). In our walk with God here and now, the Holy Spirit leads us every step of the way and He desires to help us:

- When we feel far from God, we can call on the Spirit and ask that He draw us close to Him.

- When we are troubled, we can bring our burdens to Him.

- When we are overjoyed, we can share our joy with Him.

- When we have sinned, we can ask for His forgiveness and restoration.

- When we are lost, we can cry out to Him.

The amazing reality we experience at this point in history is that not only can we now dwell with God, but God Himself dwells in us! We walk with God by virtue of the fact that we are in Him and He is in us. What an incredible gift the Spirit is in our lives! From the Fall of Adam and Eve, faithful men and women longed to enjoy just a fraction of the presence of God that we enjoy every single day. And how often do we take Him for granted?

In this journey of walking with God, we can rejoice in His presence in our lives and run to Him every step of the way. The Spirit longs to equip and empower us to experience His presence in our lives; and the very One who raised Jesus from the dead will eagerly transform us into the women and men that He created us to be as we walk with Him.

Respond

How do we, as post-resurrection believers, experience God's presence differently from people in the Old Testament?

We can go to Him anytime, anywhere

We have constant + unlimited access to God

What does it mean that God Himself is living in us through
His Holy Spirit?

_The Holy Spirit & God are
one. (+ Jesus)_

Read Galatians 5:16-26. How does the Holy Spirit's presence
impact your walk with Him?

_He leads us
in our conscience & guide -
to keep us from sinning,
making wrong choices)
- fruit of the Spirit - love, joy...
allow ourselves to be filled_

Write a prayer thanking God for sending His Spirit to guide
and direct His children, and asking Him to help you keep
pace with Him.

_Thank you God for being
relentless - for pursuing me
for fulfilling your promise
to me._

Awaiting the Joy of the Coming Kingdom: Heaven

*And I heard a loud voice from the throne saying,
"Look! God's dwelling place is now among the
people, and he will dwell with them. They will be
his people, and God himself will be with them and
be their God." Revelation 21:3*

I cannot read this passage of Revelation without welling up in tears. And as you've been following along with me on this journey through the records of history, you may understand why.

From the beginning of time, God has wanted to walk with the precious people He created. He gave Adam and Eve everything they needed to be happy, and yet they chose their own pleasure over fellowship with Him. How His heart must have ached!

Not giving up on His human creation, He promised a Messiah who would make things right. He selected a group of people to be His chosen people, through which He would show the whole world the level of intimacy He desired with everyone. But the Israelites rebelled time and time again, choosing other gods and other pleasures over the Lover of their souls. How their choices must have grieved Him!

But God was faithful in His pursuit of His beloved people, and He sent His only Son to love and rescue them. Yet the very people He came to save rejected Him and hung Him on a cross. What a travesty! How the Father must have wept.

As we saw, Jesus' story doesn't end with His death. He rose to life and ascended to heaven, where He is now seated at the right hand of the Father. He promised He's going to prepare a place for us (John 14:3), so that we can join Him where He is. From Jesus' ascension to heaven to today, we await His return.

But let's glimpse into the future, shall we? Revelation 21 gives us a beautiful picture of what we will experience when God creates a new heaven and a new earth. He will dwell among His people. He will wipe every tear from our eyes. He will erase death, mourning, crying, and pain. He will make everything new.

Magnificently, God will restore the fellowship He originally intended for us to experience with Him. This segment of history, these 8,000+ years from the Garden of Eden until Jesus returns, will be just a blip on the radar of eternity. We will spend the rest of eternity worshipping God freely, unencumbered by sin or pride or regrets. We will serve God wholeheartedly, working with joy and gladness as He gives us assignments in His kingdom. And we will walk with God blissfully, experiencing the joy of His presence eternally.

I can't wait!

Respond

What do you picture heaven is like?

I'm not sure! - beautiful creation everywhere. - nature - outside, peaceful, joyful

Read Revelation 21. Write out a few of the words that describe heaven.

holy city, new Jerusalem, no more tears, costly stone, high wall, gates (pearl), gold, clear glass, no night

It's easy to get caught up in the glitz and glamor of heaven. But read Revelation 22:3-5. What's the center focus of heaven? How will we respond?

Jesus!

What will our walk with God look like in heaven?

perfect, intimate, joyful

In what way(s) has the reading this week given you a different perspective on the narrative of the Bible and our placement in history? What are you most looking forward to in the coming kingdom of God?

No more illness, fear, guilt, complete peace + communion with God

Spend a few moments worshipping God. Thank Him for His faithfulness throughout generations, and praise Him for the certainty of our future with Him forever.

Weekend Reflection

What did you learn about God this week?

_____

_____

_____

_____

_____

_____

What did you learn about yourself this week?

_____

_____

_____

_____

_____

_____

What did you learn about walking with God this week?

_____

_____

_____

_____

_____

Write an honest prayer to God

_____

_____

_____

_____

_____

_____

Notes

Week 3:
Roadblocks to Walking with God

*Nothing teaches us about the preciousness
of the Creator as much as when we learn
the emptiness of everything else.*
— Charles Haddon Spurgeon

Reining In Our Perfectionism

*Draw near to God,
and He will draw near to you. James 4:8*

"Anything worth doing is worth doing well."

That saying has plagued me for years. It's kept me from trying new things for fear of doing them wrong. It's held me back from pursuing personal goals, because I wanted to make sure I had the perfect plan before getting started. It's become my default excuse for putting off the important things I should be doing because I felt I wasn't doing them well enough.

Perhaps the same is true for you.

Perfectionism can wreak havoc on our lives, both physical and spiritual. If we let it, it can become a roadblock in our walk with God.

But here's the thing:

It doesn't matter where you are.

It doesn't matter how religious or experienced you may be.

Frankly, God doesn't care so much what you've done in the past.

Today is always the beginning.

If you feel in your heart the yearning and desire to be close to God, to deepen your relationship with Him, to experience a whole new level of intimacy with Jesus and closeness with the Spirit, you have to do only one thing: move toward Him.

That's it. Seek Him. Take one step toward Him, whatever that looks like in your life.

Whether it's acknowledging His existence for the first time; repenting of something you know is grieving Him; setting aside a few moments every day to focus on Him; or just letting go of the shame and guilt of where you've been in the past—today take one step toward your Abba Father.

It doesn't have to be perfect. It doesn't have to be impressive. In fact, your little step may not be recorded in the annals of history. That's okay.

Because here's the truth: God is continually urging us to draw near to Him, whatever that looks like in the mess of our daily lives. And He makes this beautiful, mind-blowing promise, that if we move toward Him, He will move toward us. One little step, each and every day.

Today, if you do just one thing, if you accomplish only one thing, let it be this: that you sought the Lord with all your heart and opened yourself to the Spirit's control. God is waiting for you. He will meet you there.

Respond

This week we'll look at the roadblocks we'll face in our walk with God. List the obstacles that keep you from experiencing God's presence, whether they're related to your past, your present, your fears, or anything else.

fear of failure
not prioritizing + living intentionally
fear of not understanding
guilt over failure or fear over missed
unconfessed sin + struggles

Willingness
Awareness
Listening
Keeping Pace

(Wall Hanging)

Read Jeremiah 29:13. What does this passage say about being close to God?

When we seek God with all our heart, we will find him

Write down one way you can seek God right now.

Reading for help - prayer - giving control to him, reading my Bible

asking for His wisdom w/ my everyday responsibilities - priorities

Ask God to grow your willingness to seek Him, to help you become more aware of His presence, to <u>become more sensitive as you listen to Him</u>, and to help you keep pace as you walk with Him.

Dealing with Past Failures

Forget the former things; do not dwell on the past.
See, I am doing a new thing! Isaiah 48:18-19

Every time I start a new Bible reading plan, I get really excited.

This time is going to be different. I tell myself. *This time I'm actually going to wake up early. I'm going to set Scripture to flash on my screen when the morning alarm goes off. I'm going to keep my Bible and journal and pens in a basket so they're easy to reach. I'm going to clear off the kitchen table the night before and have everything set out ahead of time. I'm going to start drinking coffee.*

But inevitably, my best intentions fall by the wayside and I miss a day.

Then another.

And another, and then I pull it together and get back on track for a few days, only to miss another five days in a row.

If you're like me, you've also experienced the high hopes and low failures of sticking with a devotional plan. You may even wonder if reading this devotional is worth it—aren't you going to end up in the same place of failure as before?

The Israelites had experienced similar highs and lows with the Lord. Though they had every reason to be faithful to God (as we do), they would start out great but inevitably end up in sin. They didn't call on God; they didn't bring sacrifices as He had instructed them; they did not follow His commandments. But God draws their attention from their past failings to His faithfulness: "I, even I, am he who blots out your transgressions, for my own sake, and remembers your sins no more" (Isaiah 43:25).

God wanted the Israelites to <u>see their failings as an admission that they needed a Savior</u>. No matter how hard they tried, they couldn't keep God's commandments on their own. And instead of berating them for their failings, God tells them (and us) in essence, "You're right. You've failed. You can't do this. But <u>move past your failings into the righteousness that I offer you</u>. I'm doing something new and exciting, but you have to <u>let go of the past</u> and <u>embrace this new work</u> I'm going to do in you."

A [If we are to move forward in our walk with God, we can't keep looking behind us.] We must turn to face what's ahead, knowing that the One who walks beside us will be faithful to keep us close to Him.

Respond

Is it hard for you to believe that God doesn't dwell on your past failings? Why or why not?

Yes, so hard. Maybe because I focus on it so much, + because of my legalistic upbringing (church) - so shame based

Read Isaiah 43:20-28. Why do you think God tells the Israelites to "review the past" in verse 26?

to see that they needed a Savior

What do verses 26-27 mean in light of verses 18-19?

Past reminds us to look only forward at what He wants to do in our lives - only with God can we succeed + move forward

How do your past failings reveal your need for Jesus to be your righteousness?

Proof that we are nothing w/o Him - not any amount of good works can save us

What would it look like to "forget the former things" in your life and look at the new thing God is doing?

brings such a peace, calmness, assurance that He wants what is best for me + only with Him can I accomplish anything - would take away anxiety

Write a prayer asking God to help you let go of the past and believe that He is doing something new in your life.

_____
_____
_____
_____
_____
_____
_____
_____

Repenting of Our Self-Righteousness

To some who were confident of their own righteousness and looked down on everyone else, Jesus told this parable: [...] "The tax collector stood at a distance. He would not even look up to heaven, but beat his breast and said, 'God have mercy on me, a sinner.' [...] This man [...] went home justified before God."
Luke 18:9, 13-14

Those of us who grew up in church often carry both the blessings of a godly heritage and the burden of self-righteous thinking. In my own life, the Sunday School adage "Read your Bible/ Pray every day" became a way to measure spirituality instead of an act of sincere devotion.

My Bible club buddies and I memorized Bible verses, checked off reading charts, wrote down prayer lists, and did random acts of kindness. And yes, we had the common sense to go to Jesus for forgiveness, but only as a way to "cover over the gaps" in our project of self-salvation.

I would have told you that I believed in Jesus for my salvation, but in actuality I was living as my own savior, trying to impress God with my acts of righteousness, hoping to convince Him that He made a right choice in including me in His kingdom.

I was more like the Pharisees than I'd like to admit.

I often still am.

Which is why the parable of the Pharisee and the tax collector gets me every time.

God doesn't want my checklist spirituality. In fact, He despises it. It belittles the sacrifice of Jesus because it sets me up as my own savior.

What Jesus wants is a broken and contrite heart. Again and again, Jesus speaks of the joy in heaven over one sinner who repents, one sick person who acknowledges her need for a Doctor, one lost sheep who comes home, one father who says "I do believe! Help my unbelief!"

Our good deeds can become ways of avoiding Jesus as Savior when we rely on them to make ourselves feel better. We need to turn from self-justification and rest on Jesus' finished work on the cross alone for a relationship with God.

As we seek to walk with God, we must repent of our empty "righteousness" and embrace the righteousness that only He can give. Only then will we experience growing intimacy with our relationship with Him.

Respond

In what ways have you been taught that you need to "behave" in order to please God?

Church ysongin - all wells -
attendance, have losted, dressed,
served - all to "prove" I was a
good, godly Christian

Read the parable in Luke 18:9-14. Who do you most associate with in this story? Why?

depends what day you ask me (!)
Most days, I am probably subconsciously
trying to be good enough to God
even or others, or even meaning to —
to make myself feel better

Look carefully at verse 13. What does the tax collector's posture and words tell us about his heart? How does this contrast with the Pharisee?

Standing distance away, head down
shows humility + tender hearted, not
worthy, knew his place

Read Isaiah 64:6. What does this verse tell us about how God views our good works?

it's all fleeting, all like filthy
rags — but have eternal value — if done
in own own strength of wrong motives

If you were to write down the ways you try to please/impress God, what would show up on your checklist?

serving at church
hospitality to others
giving

Write a prayer repenting of your own self-righteousness and asking God to help you abandon any self-salvation projects. Thank Him for the sacrifice of Jesus, and ask Him to help you believe that His work on the cross is enough. It is finished.

_____

_____

_____

_____

_____

_____

_____

_____

Acknowledging Our Apathy

*He himself bore our sins in his body on the cross,
so that we might die to sins and live for
righteousness; by his wounds you have been healed.*
1 Peter 2:24

The more we walk with God, the more we will admire His beauty. However, too often we get so caught up in what's going on around us and what's inside us that we grow indifferent to God Himself beside us.

To combat this propensity toward apathy, we must spend regular and extended time at the cross, reminding ourselves of the travesty and the miracle that happened there.

Look back in time and see Jesus hanging on that ugly beam of wood, bearing our sins in His body, becoming sin so that we might become the righteousness of God.

See Him gasping for breath, exchanging a few precious words with criminals in His dying moments. See Him straining to pick out His mother from the crowd and placing her in John's charge so that she would be cared for. See Him looking at the Roman soldiers gambling for His clothes mere yards away, loving them instead of calling down fire from heaven to destroy them.

See Him taking in the mocking crowds, the same people who had heralded Him King mere days before, and then making this surprising plea: "Father, forgive them, for they know not what they do!" And there, to the left of the soldiers, see yourself, hurling insults with the rest of them. And Jesus looks on you with love.

The scene is revolting. It's so unfair! Why should He suffer so that those ungrateful wretches may be forgiven? Why should He die so that you and I might live?

I want to protest, to tell God that it shouldn't be this way. I want to somehow make things right, to do something so that Jesus doesn't have to take my sin on Himself. He doesn't deserve this treatment—I do!

And then it hits me.

This is grace: God gives me the forgiveness I don't deserve not just once but every day.

Sometimes, even after our salvation experience, we need to go back to Golgotha (the place of the skull) and remember. Don't rush to the tomb before you take in the great tragedy that occurred at the cross of Jesus, because you can't fully celebrate Resurrection Sunday before you've grieved Good Friday.

Let the weight of the Great Exchange fully settle into your heart. And then let it bring you to your knees as you worship the One who gave His all so that you can have all in Him.

Respond

Read John 19. Put yourself in the scene. What do you see? Hear? Taste? Feel? Look for the details in the scene. What do they say of God's attitude toward His children?

unconditional love, grace, mercy, forgiveness & resolve

Read Jesus' last conversations in the text above and in Luke 23:26-46. What do His words reveal about His heart while hanging on the cross?

heart of mercy and forgiveness;
willing to fulfill the Father's
will

Do you feel uncomfortable dwelling on the scene of the cross? Why or why not?

_No_

How does spending time at the cross influence your view of Jesus? Yourself? Your plans for the day?

keeps my focus on eternal value
and important things - not me, forces
me on Christ for the day

Respond to God in worship through reflective songs about Jesus' sacrifice on the cross. Write a prayer to God, responding to the scene of the cross.

Overcoming Our Busyness

The Lord answered her, "Martha, Martha, you
are anxious and troubled about many things, but
one thing is necessary. Mary has chosen the good
portion, which will not be taken away from her."
Luke 10:41-42

I don't know about you, but I often have the BEST
INTENTIONS to spend time with Jesus… and then life
happens. I oversleep. The laundry pile overflows. That bank
transfer doesn't go through. And we're out of milk.

Before I know it, those few moments I would have spent
with God have vanished into thin air and the rest of my day
becomes a marathon of putting out fires.

I'm glad God included the story of Martha and Mary in the
Bible, because I can relate. Martha was overwhelmed with
everything she needed to do to get dinner on the table for 13
hungry men, and Mary was hanging out at the feet of Jesus,
oblivious to the chaos in the kitchen. I totally get Martha. I
expect my family to pitch in and work together when we have
company over for dinner. And like Martha, much of my life is
spent worried and bothered by many things.

In the midst of this bedlam, Jesus called Martha to live
centered in the only thing that matters—her relationship with
Him. Jesus wasn't condemning Martha's culinary activity;
after all, the meal had to be served one way or another. But in
the midst of all the preparations, Martha lost sight of the One
seated in her living room, just as we can get so preoccupied
with our daily lives that we forget the One we're walking
beside.

John 11:20

But before we despair, there is hope for all us "Marthas," ruled by the tyranny of the urgent. The next time Martha appears in the Bible, she had learned her lesson of prioritizing Jesus above her to-do list. Having just buried her brother, she left the mourners at her house and ran to Jesus when He came to town, while Mary lagged behind (John 11:20). This time, Martha brought her concerns to Him instead of pouting about them, and in return she received clarity about her situation, peace in her heart, and hope anew when Jesus brought Lazarus back to life.

Dear friends, let us learn to become aware of His presence in the midst of the chaos. Time with God is not something we fit in between the chores and errands—it is a continual conversation as we bring the everyday stuff of life to Him.

We are not too busy to spend time with God because God is right there in the midst of our busyness. He's just waiting for us to acknowledge Him, and His presence will bring peace to any situation.

Respond

Read Luke 10:38-42. Can you relate to Martha?

Oh yes!

In what ways have you been too busy to spend time with God?

Just to much on my plate in general — not organized enough, or purposeful enough

What does Jesus' response teach us about His character and
His desire for us?

He is patient in his response,
kind, gentle but firm in
showing Martha what is
truly important

Read John 11:17-44. How does this story of Martha's
interaction with Jesus give you hope?

Second chances - Jesus always
responds to us, when we come to
him, no matter how much we mess up

In what ways can acknowledge God's presence throughout
the day instead of waiting for the "right time" and the "right
place" to spend time with God?

Pray as we go about our day -
always asking for guidance
→ always praising him in
the little things

Write a prayer asking God to help you prioritize the one
thing that is important in life and to become increasingly
aware of His presence in your life.

Weekend Reflection

What did you learn about God this week?

_____
_____
_____
_____
_____
_____

What did you learn about yourself this week?

_____
_____
_____
_____
_____
_____

What did you learn about walking with God this week?

_____
_____
_____
_____

Write an honest prayer to God

_____
_____
_____
_____
_____
_____

Notes

_____

_____

_____

_____

_____

_____

_____

_____

_____

_____

_____

_____

_____

_____

_____

_____

_____

_____

_____

_____

_____

_____

_____

_____

_____

_____

Week 4:
Rhythms of Walking with God

*Whoever says he abides in Jesus ought to
walk in the same way in which he walked.*
— 1 John 2:6

Bowing Everything to Him: Worship

In your presence is fullness of joy;
In your right hand there are pleasures forever.
Psalm 16:11 (NASB)

As we walk with God, we quickly learn that certain practices help us grow closer to Him. Historically, the church called these practices spiritual disciplines, and they provided Christians rhythm to their spiritual lives. To this day, these disciplines help us experience a deeper awareness of God's presence because they remind us of who we are and who God is.

The moment we take our eyes off of Jesus and forget His sacrifice, we slip into apathy, wandering from the source of Life and trying to do things our own way. But Christ's love compels us, it moves us, it transforms us from hollow people who only speak of God from our lips to people overflowing with the joy and love of God, grabbing hold of the abundant life that is really life.

In my own journey of walking with God, I've learned that worship is the first spiritual discipline that recalibrates my entire view of life. When I come back to the cross and begin praising God for all He is, His mercies inundate my heart and remind me what life is really about. Worship is both a moment of bowing my heart before God and a lifestyle of bowing my actions before Him as well.

When we taste and see that the Lord is good, our entire lives become symphonies of praise back to Him. He fills us with

His living water and our lives become overflowing wells that spill His grace and love into the lives of our families and friends. His song is continually in our mouths, whether we're experiencing our dreams come true or our world is crashing down around us.

Worship is a sacrifice of praise. It means not just singing a few songs and going my merry way but presenting my body, my mind, and my obedience to God. It is a glorious transformation that takes place in the little moments of life, sweeping Cheerios off the floor, getting out of the warm bed to seek Him, smiling at the rude cashier, or serving the last piece of cake instead of eating it myself.

And in these little moments of worship seen only by the Father, we discover His presence all around us and His joy filling us.

Respond

What does worship mean to you?

Corporate always comes to mind first, but more its a constant state I put my mind + body in throughout the day - praising God for the good + hard things that happen, thankfulness, communion w/ Him

Read Psalm 16:11 again. How is worship described in this passage?

being in His presence - joy, pleasures forever. Him making himself known to us + His path for us

How is worship both a moment of bowing our hearts to God and a lifestyle of bowing our lives to God?

Bowing our heart in a moment - needed to get ourselves in a right state of mind - getting our heart right so he can worship - lifestyle - then it can become a lifestyle - a part of everything we to things that our joy - continual bowing of our heart

How does worship bring our hearts in line with God's and help us stay in step with the Spirit?

Well, we are putting ourselves in a right position for worship, worship keeps our focus on Him gets focus off the negative & what God wants from us instead

Today, take 10 minutes to simply praise God for who He is and what He has done. Then present yourself and your day to Him as a sacrifice of praise, and ask Him to teach you how to worship with your life and not just your lips. You may be surprised by the results.

Worship with my life not just my lips

Testing Our Loyalties: Fasting

How sweet are your words to my taste,
sweeter than honey to my mouth.
Psalm 119:103

I don't know about you, but I've had a pretty rocky relationship with fasting.

Growing up, my family would fast until 3 p.m. every Good Friday, and I thought it was some way of showing God just how sad we were about Jesus' death. Then in high school, I heard that God wants us to fast in order to grow in our relationship with Him, so I abstained from all food every Tuesday my sophomore and junior year. Then later I was told that we should fast before big decisions, so I fasted while deciding where to go to college and who to marry.

And while all those reasons may be valid motives to fast, for years I missed the main one: fasting tests our loyalties and reveals the true desires of our hearts. One of the easiest ways to tell what really controls us is to give up something we relish and watch our reaction. I didn't think I had a sugar addiction or a Facebook problem until I fasted from them; I soon realized they both had a greater hold on my life than I would have wanted to admit.

God wants us to be undivided in our devotion for Him. He wants us to run to Him with our problems, not seek to drown them in a pint of ice cream. He wants us to seek Him in our spare moments, not waste them on social media. He wants us to look for approval and affirmation in Him, not depend on our makeup. He wants us to find our security in Him, not rely on the numbers in our bank account.

In our walks with God, we will encounter numerous temptations that seek to draw our hearts from Him. The best way to put these temptations to rest is to fast from them and declare to our God, "This much, oh God, I want you! More than food. More than money. More than constant connection. More than anything else that threatens to put a wedge between us. Nothing is more precious to me than You, and I'm willing to give up whatever it takes to draw closer to You."

Those are heavy words, friends, and there's pain in the initial separation as we wean our hearts off of these would-be-gods that tempt us with their pleasures.

But the rewards far outweigh the cost. We give up momentary pleasures and gain everlasting riches in God. We trade empty shells of promises for the heavenly riches in Christ Jesus. We exchange slavery to our lusts and passions for freedom in Christ. We turn away from the siren's call to death and destruction and walk toward the fullness of life that is truly life.

This is the kind of fasting that God calls us to. And this is the kind of fasting that will help us say, with the psalmist, "How sweet are Your words to my taste, sweeter than honey to my mouth."

Respond

Read Matthew 6:17-18. What does this passage say about the rewards of fasting?

Should be done in secret so that God will reward you — not noticed by men

How can fasting deepen your relationship with God?

helps you realize what your strongholds are and helps focus on what really matters — freedom in Christ, relationship with Him

Rewrite Psalm 119:103 in your own words, replacing "honey" with the habits or temptations that have encroached on your relationship with God.

How sweet are your words to my taste! Yes, sweeter than coffee & my mouth! "sugar"

What would it look like to fast from them to test whether they're an innocent pleasure or a controlling addiction?

A bit scary

Spend a few minutes in prayer, asking God to show you whether you need to fast from anything for a season. Then write a prayer in response to your conversation with Him.

_____

_____

_____

_____

_____

_____

_____

Loving God in Daily Life: Serving

*Whatever you do, whether in word or deed, do it
all in the name of the Lord Jesus. [...] It is the
Lord Christ you are serving. Colossians 3:17, 24*

One of the greatest joys of walking with God is the privilege
of being used by Him to serve others. The world doesn't see
God, but it sees us, and we get to be His hands and feet,
touching the lives of those we interact with as He looks on
with a big grin.

Every little thing we do in Jesus' Name and for His sake
matters. Every single one. There is no task too small—even a
cup of water given in love blesses His heart. If we want to
show God we love Him, we can start by loving those around
us.

It's tempting to think of some work as more holy than other
work. After all, doesn't God consider delivering meals to the
needy as more important than serving mac & cheese to our
own kids? Actually, no. According to Colossians 3:17, 24 all
work done in His Name pleases Him, whether we're
sweeping the floors or leading the church choir, buying
groceries or serving the homeless, presenting reports at the
office or studying the Bible.

Doing something in His Name means acknowledging Him as
Lord in that situation, working *for* Him (not our boss), *through*
Him (not our own ambition), and *to* Him (not ourselves). It
means recognizing that "all things were created by Him and
for Him. He is before all things and in Him all things hold
together… so that in everything He might have the
supremacy" (Colossians 1:16-19). When we bow our actions

and our service before God, He uses those humble acts of obedience to bless the world in ways we cannot even fathom.

When we learn to see our work as part of our walk with God, we will spend less time worrying about "God's will for our lives" and more time being faithful right where He has placed us. And in those moments of faithful serving, we will experience His presence in ways we never could while seated on the sofa with our Bibles and coffee.

God is real. He is active. He is on the move. And when we join Him in what He is doing in the world by being faithful where He has placed us, we will see Him do great things as we walk with Him.

Respond

Read Colossians 3:17, 24. What does this passage say about our work?

Everything we do - big or little - is noticed by God and it need to do it for Him, to our best ability, everything we do in His name matters

How can we walk with God and experience His pleasure when we're about our daily business?

By doing everything with thankfulness, giving our best to Him - knowing He is pleased even by the mundane if its done in His name. It brings me joy knowing that what I do is bringing him joy - knowing He is pleased with me

Read 2 Corinthians 5:14-15. How can you live for God right where He has placed you?

By doing everything out of love for Him - live my life, right where I am, to love + please + honor God. Learn to see our self as part of our walk with God.

Whatever your primary occupation--whether an analyst on Wall Street, a production line worker in a factory, a stay-at-home mom, a waitress in a mom-and-pop shop, a prison warden, or anything else--give your job to Jesus today and ask Him to show you what it means to work in His Name. Ask Him to give you an increased awareness of His presence in your life during the mundane tasks of your day, and ask Him to help you serve others around your with His love.

Talking with God: Prayer

Devote yourselves to prayer. Colossians 4:2

The car lunged to a stop and my eyes shot open in fear, the tempting aroma of burgers and fries quickly forgotten when I realized my mom was blessing the food while navigating traffic. I was certain we were going to die, or at the very least, God wouldn't bless our food, because as a nine-year-old, I assumed we had to pray with our heads bowed, eyes closed, and hands clasped together.

That day I learned an important lesson: God hears our prayers regardless of what posture we adopt, what words we use, where we are, or what we're doing. In fact, He longs for us to be in constant communication with Him, to connect our spirit to His in prayer.

Obviously, for this to happen, prayer needs to look different from what we were used to as children. As we mature, our understanding of prayer and communion with God should mature as well.

We need to set aside time for focused prayer, when we go into a secret place, close the door, and wrestle in prayer (Matthew 6:6). We will also experience great blessings when praying with two or three other believers, bringing requests before God and agreeing in prayer (Matthew 18:19). And praying before meals and bedtime is a wonderful practice that reminds us to be thankful. But if these types of prayer times are the only conversation with God we experience, we are missing out.

God wants us to constantly talk to and listen to Him. Throughout the day, He longs for us to direct our thoughts and hearts toward Him, acknowledging His presence right beside us.

- Good news? Praise God.

- Bad news? Ask God.

- Problem? Seek God.

- Sin? Repent before God.

- Unexpected blessing? Thank God.

- Burden? Bring it to God.

As we learn to direct our hearts toward Him and converse with Him throughout our day, <u>we will also begin to hear Him respond to us</u>. Sometimes with a Bible verse. Sometimes with lyrics from a song. Sometimes through the words of a stranger.

By developing a spirit of constant prayer, we begin to notice God's daily presence in our lives. And life takes on new layers of depth and meaning when we walk in step with the Spirit in prayer.

Respond

Read Ephesians 6:18. What does this passage say about prayer?

To pray at all times
— in the spirit

How can we pray at all times?

_____

_____

_____

_____

Write a prayer asking God to help you listen to Him and talk
with Him throughout your day.

_____

_____

_____

_____

_____

_____

_____

_____

_____

It can take time to get into the habit of constantly conversing
with God. Try to tie this new habit to a daily routine: have a
short talk with God whenever you wash your hands or reach
a stoplight. Or, alternatively, set an alarm on your phone
throughout the day to remind you to and pause to talk to
God about what's happening. With time, constant prayer will
become second nature and you will become more proficient
in listening and hearing Him.

Feasting on Our Daily Bread: Bible Study

Let the Word of Christ dwell in you richly.
Colossians 3:16

The Word of God is powerful, and those who have personal copies of the Bible own a commodity that millions of people throughout history have only ever dreamed of. Even now, there are Christians around the world who do not own a Bible. Meanwhile, my shelves are lined with so many translations and editions of the Bible, and I haven't even read them all. Perhaps this is true for you as well. On top of all these, we have a plethora of Bible apps on our phones, sermons at our fingertips, worship songs on radio stations, and Christian literature just a click away.

We live in an age of biblical affluence. If God's Word was bread on our tables, we sit down to feast on a bounty, while others around the world scamper for a few crumbs here and there. And like picky toddlers, too often we push away from the table, too stuffed with worldly pleasures to hunger for plain bread, too bothered to pick up a loaf.

What are we doing with the abundance of God's Word at our fingertips?

Yes, we should consume the Bible with voracious appetites. But I'm not talking about simply reading a chapter of the Bible and checking it off our lists. God's Word must live in us, powerfully transforming us from the inside out. When we study the Bible, we grow to know and love God more as we discover Him on the pages of Scripture. And the more we learn about God's character as revealed in Scripture, the more quickly we will recognize His voice when He speaks to us.

Remember that God doesn't call us to Bible reading plans. He calls us to Christ-in-us living, as the Word of God, Jesus Christ Himself, dwells richly in us. We must soak in His Word so that it penetrates our hearts and transforms our actions.

Whether we spend two hours or two minutes, let us take time to sit down and feast at the table of God's Word. Let us approach the Bible with open hearts and eager expectation to hear from Him, and let us ask that the Living Word of God continue to dwell in us long after we shut the cover of our Bibles.

Respond

Read Hebrews 4:12. What does this passage say about God's Word?

_____

_____

_____

_____

How have you experienced the power of God's Word in your life?

_____

_____

_____

_____

Read John 1:1-2, 14. This passage refers to Jesus as God's Word. How is this different from the way we typically understand God's Word as words bound in a book? In what ways is Jesus God's Word?

_____

_____

_____

How does the reality of Jesus as God's Word change your understanding of Hebrews 4:12 and Colossians 3:16?

_____

_____

_____

In what ways can the Word of God dwell in us during the time when we're not studying the Bible?

_____

_____

_____

In what ways can you be filled with the Word of God by using the variety of resources at your disposal? Get creative, and write down one specific way you will feast on God's Word this week and experience His presence in your life.

_____

_____

_____

_____

_____

Weekend Reflection

What did you learn about God this week?

_____
_____
_____
_____
_____
_____

What did you learn about yourself this week?

_____
_____
_____
_____
_____
_____

What did you learn about walking with God this week?

_____
_____
_____
_____
_____

Write an honest prayer to God

_____
_____
_____
_____
_____
_____

Notes

_____

_____

_____

_____

_____

_____

_____

_____

_____

_____

_____

_____

_____

_____

_____

_____

_____

_____

_____

_____

_____

_____

_____

_____

_____

_____

_____

_____

_____

_____

_____

Conclusion

As we've journeyed together through the past four weeks, I hope your understanding of walking with God has grown with each passing day, even as you have experienced more of His presence in your life.

I love the imagery of walking with God because it reflects the fact that this relationship is dynamic, constantly moving and going places. My relationship with God deepens each season, as He reveals new and fresh mercies in my life.

With the Spirit as our Guide, our walks will never get boring.

- He will increase our *Willingness* to walk with Him on uncharted trails.

- He will increase our *Awareness* of His presence in ways we had never known before.

- He will increase our capacity to *Listen* to Him in ways we had never heard before.

- He will increase our ability to *Keep pace* with Him as we speed up and take sharp turns to new places.

Walking with God is the adventure of a lifetime, and it's one that gets more exciting the closer we grow to Him. Through the valleys and on the hilltops, He will be with us, guiding us every step of the way until He leads us safely Home.

May you enjoy every step of the journey, as you learn to walk with Him.

Many blessings,

Asheritah

About the Author

Asheritah Ciuciu is a writer and speaker. She grew up in Romania as a missionary kid and studied English and Women's Ministry at Cedarville University in Ohio. Her passion is helping women find joy in Jesus through a deeper walk with God, and she shares vulnerably from her own life experiences on www.OneThingAlone.com. She is married to Flaviu, a web programmer and artist, and together they raise their spunky children in beautiful Northeast Ohio.

FREE ECOURSE!

Get it straight in your inbox

ENROLL TODAY

To say thank you for buying this book,
I'd like to give you an eCourse 100% free.

Just go to
www.onethingalone.com/daily-devotions-ecourse
to enroll today.

one thing alone

FINDING JOY IN JESUS

Connect with Asheritah Ciuciu
and sign up for announcements and upcoming titles:

www.onethingalone.com

- blog

- speaking events

- Scripture Art

- free downloads

- and more!

facebook.com/onethingalone

@asheritah

Made in the USA
Middletown, DE
05 March 2018